ELECTING A KENNEDY CONGRESS

Forming A Government Which Will Support RFK Jr's Efforts To Remake America in Its Own Image

by

John Rachel

Published by
Literary Vagabond Books
Los Angeles • Osaka

literaryvagabond.com

Electing A Kennedy Congress:
Forming A Government Which Will
Support RFK Jr's Efforts to Remake
America in Its Own Image
Copyright © 2023
by John Rachel

ISBN #979-8-861-02398-6

Cover Art by Peter Maximilian Crenshaw.

Table of Contents

Introduction

The debacle which occurred in the House of Representatives on July 20, 2023 is frightening, illustrative, and a giant wake-up call. Our political class is a collection of petty mediocrities, lacking principles and perspective. They are third rate actors reading from a horrible script, ruthless and self-serving to the core, drunk on power, loyal only to their deep-pocketed patrons, unmindful of how they turn an historically momentous, socially vital, and economically crucial institution of governance, into a cheap charade, an insult to the brilliant vision of the Founding Fathers and to common decency.

First, the pre-session attempt by 104 members of the Democratic Party to prevent RFK Jr from even appearing, barring a person who probably has more of value to say than all of them combined, to censor him from a HEARING ON CENSORSHIP, was a cruel and surrealistic irony. Then to see the contempt Mr. Kennedy was treated with, especially by his own political party, is proof what a hammerlock the establishment oligarchy has on the legislative branch of our government. In their view, RFK Jr challenges way too many of the official ruling dictums to even be allowed to share and properly explain his views, much less having those views be given fair and objective consideration. The gatekeepers demand that he be humiliated, denigrated, discredited, and ultimately shunned.

His prospects for election don't just run up against resistance. They confront the headwinds of ruthless, merciless, hateful opposition, bad actors who will settle for nothing less than his complete destruction as a political force, regardless of the merits or popularity of what he advocates. Voters are to be categorically denied the opportunity to vote for him. End of story.

Yet that's not even the essential predicament his candidacy faces. That's not the deal-breaker anyone rooting for the kinds of sweeping changes he is proposing, crucially needs to understand, appreciate, and decisively address.

Let's say that RFK Jr wins the election by an impressive margin, if not a landslide. But the vast majority of those now holding House and Senate seats are returned to Washington DC.

Here's what is tragically inevitable. And what we must acknowledge.

As Robert F. Kennedy, Jr. attempts to push through his laudable agenda, we will witness the most colossal political cage fight in U.S. history. It will be gridlock to the power of ten. Kennedy's own corrupt Democratic Party will do everything within their power – and they most certainly have the leverage – to sabotage every one of RFK Jr's initiatives. He will constantly be confronted, harassed and vilified. His noble and much-needed attempts to work constructively with other nations, for example with Russia and China, will be condemned as treason. His ideas on raising the standard of living of everyday

Americans at best labeled untimely, at worst quixotic lunacy. His revamping of the entire approach the U.S. takes to health care will be vandalized. His paradigm-shifting goal of reining in corporate power – particularly that of big pharma, agrichemical, the defense industry – curtailing excessive corporate influence in deciding national policy, will be declared dead on arrival.

It wouldn't surprise me if immediately after RFK Jr took the oath of office for the presidency, the House established a permanent, working House Committee for Impeachment of the President, to issue a steady stream of investigations, accusations and formal indictments of him, then the same for whoever his vice-presidential running mate ends up being, once the kangaroo impeachment proceedings successfully remove RFK Jr from office.

This brings into sharp focus the entire purpose of this book.

If we don't take anything else from the July 20 hearing and the constant stream of invective being disgorged by the media as this book goes to press, we must totally commit ourselves to this call to action:

WE MUST ELECT A KENNEDY CONGRESS IN 2024!

Otherwise, RFK Jr's laudable agenda and courageous campaign for the presidency will just end up as a minor footnote in history.

The Subtitle

We know what Robert F. Kennedy, Jr. stands for. We know what kind of America he envisions. We understand how his commitment to all Americans, not just the rich and powerful, was shaped by his father and both of his uncles. We could say – though I don't mean to sound trite – the "Kennedy brand" is very familiar to anyone who knows U.S. history from the 60s on.

Our country has had many remarkable individuals from the political left. Some whom immediately come to mind: Robert LaFollette, Henry Wallace, Jacob Javits, Adam Clayton Powell Jr., Bella Abzug, George McGovern, John Conyers, John Lewis, Ted Kennedy, Paul Wellstone, and Dennis Kucinich.

What do we have now? We have the diluted, tepid faux progressives in the persons of Eleanor Roosevelt-cosplayer Elizabeth Warren and bass player Beto O'Rourke. We have the controlled opposition of The Squad, led by lipstick ad princess AOC, who once served coffee and apple pie as a waitress and now just as obsequiously serves oligarch-in-residence Nancy Pelosi. And of course, we have Bernie. Unfortunately, when this beautiful, inspiring man had a majority of the country behind him and his agenda and was handed an opportunity to change the disastrous course we've been on for decades, he folded his cards and fell back in line, judging he could best serve the country as a team player. He sold out to the establishment so he could maintain his position of influence in the Senate for the final chapters of his career in that august body of lapdogs. He walked away from an opportunity to make history which only arrives a few times each century. It was a sad day for our nation, indeed. A disheartening tragedy.

Things have just continued to deteriorate.

Let me offer just one emblematic example of the abysmal state of moral leadership in Congress: There's not a single one of these self-aggrandizing congressional virtue signalers calling for world peace. If Congress were a rock band, it would be called The Warmongers.

What are we supposed to make of a "left" – and I have to use quotation marks because the entire concept has been gutted of any cogent meaning – that is pro-war and willing to sacrifice the welfare of the citizenry and risk nuclear annihilation to build an empire of tyranny across the globe?

The condition of progressive politics is pathetic and mortifying!

What other conclusion is there? The congressional left is now a collection of Muppets which delivers lip service and pleasant-sounding word salad in spades, but no real action. It's a mime troupe which inspires more pause than confidence that anything will get done to benefit the majority of citizens.

Now here's the kicker!

Somehow, despite the sham that our democracy has become; regardless of the total abandonment of everyday people and abject failure to serve the interests of 99% of its citizens; despite the abysmal poverty of countless Americans, crumbling of infrastructure, and accelerating economic decline; notwithstanding the blatant censorship, suppression of free speech and political dissent in America and across the media landscape it controls; in spite of the 24/7 illegal surveillance of innocent individuals, heavy-handed policing and the outlandish incarceration rate, especially of people of color; in the face of America's squandering its vast natural and human resources in pursuit of world domination; despite all of that, the U.S. has somehow maintained its image as the standard-bearer of all sorts of laudable, wonderful values. This applies to brainwashed folks – arguably a clear majority – both within its borders and across the globe. Allegedly we stand for freedom, justice, equality, peace, respect for human rights and personal dignity, equal opportunity, free speech, freedom of the press, respect for international law, the list goes on. The official narrative would have it that great, benevolent, generous, charitable, wise and compassionate nation that we are, America spreads "democracy and freedom" to other countries all over the world – whether they want it or not – even though when it takes root, it strangely looks more like tyranny than democratic self-determination by the people. It's frankly mind-boggling and impossible to understand how, in light of U.S. bullying, aggression, perpetual war – America has been at war 235 years of its 243 years as a nation – the chaos it seeds across the planet, the sanctions it imposes on other nations causing starvation and death, its inability to ever admit a mistake, its complete aversion to working cooperatively with any other nation, that other people look at the U.S. with anything other than horror and contempt. Then again, like they say in advertising: image is everything.

That "image" of a good, wholesome, trustworthy, and wonderful America, beacon of hope and light, is what RFK Jr intends to reestablish. Implied is that we should on blind faith believe that it once existed here. Whether it did or not is a moot point. Because whether we as a nation, society, or system of government ever lived up to it or not, it represents an ideal. An ideal which has inspired millions of individuals, both in the U.S. and elsewhere, to dream of, yearn for, and put their lives on the line to become "like us".

That image of America as a good force in the world is certainly what vast numbers of American citizens want to believe is true.

This is what is behind the sub-title of this book, specifically the phrase 'remake America in its own image'. It's a call to action to do what I see is necessary to remake our faltering, dysfunctional nation into what many of us naively believe it already is, but more importantly, what we loyal, patriotic citizens want America to stand for, to represent, to symbolize, to embrace.

To be!

As RFK Jr himself says on his campaign website:

> "America was once an inspiration to the world, a beacon of freedom and democracy. Our priority will be nothing less than to restore our moral leadership. We will lead by example."

For far too long, the U.S. has propped up a false image of itself, conned the world, abused the trust and faith that image triggers inside and outside its borders. It's time for America to stop playing games, stop fabricating fairy tales and indefensible fantasies, and begin truly living up to that priceless image, proudly and with unshakeable commitment.

Remember: Every lie has a shelf life. The lies that the U.S. is a force of good and wants peace, and a host of other post-WWII propaganda fictions, reached their expiration dates when the Cold War ended in 1992 with the collapse of the Soviet Union, if not before. Those onerous, stale, noxious lies must end and be replaced with a reality – a noble and inspiring set of truths – as we unite and remake our country into the nation we can with an open heart and clean conscience, believe in again.

D is for Disconnect

I didn't meet a Republican until I was 18 years old, my freshman year at university. I grew up in working class suburbs of Detroit. Everyone was union. Everyone was a Democrat. This was the party of the New Deal, FDR, JFK.

That political party, that institution which understood and worked for everyday people – the blue collars of the lower class and the white collars of the middle class – that political force which invested its energy to foster an America for all, to serve the citizenry equally regardless of class status, the party which took seriously the constitutional mandate "to promote the general welfare", no longer exists.

The transition took place during the 90s under the saxophone president, Bill Clinton, and was complete by the turn of the century. No longer was the Democratic Party a party of the people. It ended up serving the same monied class as the Republicans. As Ralph Nader puts it, choice at the polls now was deciding between Tweedledee and Tweedledum.

Democrats currently wonder why party loyalty has been diminishing, why Hillary Clinton lost to a glib reality show host/gambling casino magnate in 2016, a manifestly dishonest, terminally shallow, narcissistic, manipulative, self-serving, completely unqualified candidate in Donald Trump. It's not difficult to explain: The new Democratic Party is the party which railroaded one of the most popular candidates in recent history, Bernie Sanders, out of the race, stranding the largest populous uprising in decades.

As if that weren't insulting enough, Hillary made no secret of her disdain for the "deplorables" of America, the unwashed masses who didn't benefit from pedigree educations, bulging stock portfolios, and natty wardrobes from Prada and Armani. Her elitist predilection was then reinforced by the leak of a speech she gave to top banking executives, where she claimed she had "both a public and private position" on Wall Street reform. The execs got the real story and the voting public was served up the usual campaign blather. Is it any wonder that her bid for the presidency was crippled by plummeting trust?

To his credit, Trump said many of the right things which resonated with the masses of voters alienated by the new corporate trimmings of the DNC and its penchant for supporting centrist establishment-friendly candidates. To his discredit, Trump apparently didn't mean what he said and managed to avoid fulfilling most of the promises he made in his campaign. But it was too late. And it's still too late. Huge numbers of frustrated and angry voters are so fed up with the tone-deaf Democratic Party, they seem to be willing to forgive Trump for just about anything. We shouldn't do what the Dems did in 2016 and underestimate the Orange Oligarch. Because he is perhaps the most gifted smooth talker to come down the pike since 'Slick Willy'. Fool me twice.

Of course, the Democrats couldn't leave it at just being disconnected from flesh-and-blood entities – the voting public, real life people. They made the existential leap of disconnecting from reality itself. I refer to Russiagate.

I'm not going to get into the messy details of this scam. As there are still folks out there who believe the Earth is flat, there are a frightening number of individuals who believe that Russia, in collusion with KGB mole Drumpf – code name Agent Orange – stole the election from the universally-adored Hillary and dropped it off at the Mar-a-Lago clubhouse. Many of these folks also think that Saddam Hussein attacked the Twin Towers, Iraq had nuclear bombs ready to lob at the Lincoln Memorial and on Disney World, and the space shuttle tiles are oven-crisp taco shells.

Suffice it to say, the ham-fisted subterfuge created to cover Hillary's embarrassing electoral failure has, to put it mildly, created extensive collateral damage. Granted, the project to disappear Russia as a nation, dismember it, and parcel it into manageable chunks for maximum exploitation, already had legs, thanks to the PNAC neoconiacs. However, Russiagate went the extra mile in convincing most of the U.S. population that Vladimir Putin is a Hitlerian monster, and Russia a backward, malevolent, evil, ruthless, genocidal gas station masquerading as a country, bent on destroying America and forcing us all to listen to balalaika music 24 hours a day. Subsequent loathing lasting right up to the present for both Putin and everything Russian – now at warp speed with the Ukraine meatgrinder in full swing – has been meticulously built on the sludgerock foundation of the DNC/Hillary Clinton Russiagate propaganda. Slanderous attacks, whole-cloth fabrications about the sinister Putin and revanchist Russian war machine continue to spew out 24/7. Questioning this baseless vitriol is equated with treason. Both sides of the congressional aisle scream for blood – Russian blood – and the prospects for WWIII are real and terrifying!

Not that such mass psychosis is anything new. Manufactured crisis is one product line we haven't off shored to China. It's a nefarious web of deceptions at which our own Deep State excels. Which is why the U.S. never runs out of enemies and why it's always at war. Our Nobel Peace Prize president was actively engaged in military conflict with seven countries. Obama dropped 26,171 bombs on foreign soil, just his final year in office. A "peace time" record?

Assuring the public that we're not wasting tax dollars, that as global policeman, we're killing people who really deserve it, that we're eliminating serious threats to the security of America, that we're "fighting them over there so we don't end up fighting them here," is a lot of work and not always as easy as it looks. Nothing reflecting favorably on the "enemy" can be allowed. America's vile nemesis must be marginalized, dehumanized, demonized. Their leaders must be portrayed as devils, Hitlers, evil incarnate. The evil country, its citizens, its leadership, its democracy-hating government must be blamed for every mishap, no matter how unrelated. Experts must offer ever more outrageous prognostications about what nefarious plans said enemy is conjuring in order to inflict more horrors on the U.S. and its loyal allies.

With a lot of practice, the U.S. propaganda machine has gotten very good at all of this. For example, the day after Russia started its special military operation to eliminate the growing military threat NATO was creating in Ukraine, we were instructed – and dutifully did our patriotic duty by enthusiastically complying – to hate Russian music, dance, art, literature, sports figures. Even Russian cats and dogs were barred from appearing in pet shows in the West. Western businesses based in Russia packed up and left, losing billions of dollars, rather than be around those despicable, foul, savage Russians. Air space was closed to any aircraft or carrier that had any affiliation with Russia. Offices of Russian media outlets in the West were shut down. It was truly the most viciously thorough campaign of cultural genocide in recent history. And yes, U.S. citizens have in hordes stepped up to the plate and carried their weight. Saying anything even moderately nice about Russia in America – especially Vladimir Putin – risks at minimum a barrage of expletives, a possible beating, even gunshot wounds. Order a White Russian from a bartender at your own risk.

'Hate' like 'love' is a four-letter word. But apparently the former is a much easier sell. Or perhaps, considering the frustrations and anger which seem to be mounting as chaos and dysfunction in everyday life become more the norm, people were and are uniquely primed for some heavy-duty animus.

It's a truly disheartening comment on human nature.

One final point.

Like Anthrax spores, hatred is almost impossible to put back in the bottle. It's contagious and grows exponentially. We hate Russia, we hate North Korea, we hate Assad of Syria, we hate the Ayatollah of Iran, we hate Cuba, we hate Venezuela. We need to hate China much more. Yes, we're lagging a little in that department. After all … Covid-19, communism, TikTok.

The problem is, hate knows no borders. Inevitably, it comes back home. Now we see the acid-drip is corroding the vital fabric of American society. The Democrats hate Trump. Republicans hate Biden. MSNBC viewers hate Fox viewers. The vaccinated hate the unvaccinated. Of course, all enlightened people are derelict if they don't hate haters. Haters would be anyone who is a transphobe, homophobe, racist, a racism denier, anti-Semite, an anti-Semitism denier, anyone who questions the positive impact of BLM and MRNA vaccines or the necessity of internet censorship, puberty blockers for children, 5G, 3-D printed meat, or 80+ genders. No reason to talk to any of these people. Just hate them.

By the way, as haters of all that should be hated, we should be proud we live in the most democratic, wealthiest, most powerful, most just and free nation in history! Because God is on our side, and we are chosen by destiny to rule the entire known universe. Everything we do is good and wonderful.

Yes, this is how disconnect works. It operates by its own rules, has no time for muddling distractions like facts, logic, reason, objectivity, respectful debate, historical perspective, common sense, common decency, love of truth.

D is for disconnect.

D is for deception.

D is for dystopia.

R is for Regressive

Here is the U.S. Federal Income Tax Rate Schedule from 1963.

Historical U.S. Federal Individual Income Tax Rates and Brackets

Year	Married Filing Jointly		Married Filing Separately		Single Filer	
	Rates	Brackets	Rates	Brackets	Rates	Brackets
1963	20.0% >	$0	20.0% >	$0	20.0% >	$0
	22.0% >	$4,000	22.0% >	$2,000	22.0% >	$2,000
	26.0% >	$8,000	26.0% >	$4,000	26.0% >	$4,000
	30.0% >	$12,000	30.0% >	$6,000	30.0% >	$6,000
	34.0% >	$16,000	34.0% >	$8,000	34.0% >	$8,000
	38.0% >	$20,000	38.0% >	$10,000	38.0% >	$10,000
	43.0% >	$24,000	43.0% >	$12,000	43.0% >	$12,000
	47.0% >	$28,000	47.0% >	$14,000	47.0% >	$14,000
	50.0% >	$32,000	50.0% >	$16,000	50.0% >	$16,000
	53.0% >	$36,000	53.0% >	$18,000	53.0% >	$18,000
	56.0% >	$40,000	56.0% >	$20,000	56.0% >	$20,000
	59.0% >	$44,000	59.0% >	$22,000	59.0% >	$22,000
	62.0% >	$52,000	62.0% >	$26,000	62.0% >	$26,000
	65.0% >	$64,000	65.0% >	$32,000	65.0% >	$32,000
	69.0% >	$76,000	69.0% >	$38,000	69.0% >	$38,000
	72.0% >	$88,000	72.0% >	$44,000	72.0% >	$44,000
	75.0% >	$100,000	75.0% >	$50,000	75.0% >	$50,000
	78.0% >	$120,000	78.0% >	$60,000	78.0% >	$60,000
	81.0% >	$140,000	81.0% >	$70,000	81.0% >	$70,000
	84.0% >	$160,000	84.0% >	$80,000	84.0% >	$80,000
	87.0% >	$180,000	87.0% >	$90,000	87.0% >	$90,000
	89.0% >	$200,000	89.0% >	$100,000	89.0% >	$100,000
	90.0% >	$300,000	90.0% >	$150,000	90.0% >	$150,000
	91.0% >	$400,000	91.0% >	$200,000	91.0% >	$200,000

Back then, if your gross income was $4,000 or less, you paid a 20% rate. If your gross income was $400,000 or more, on the earnings over $400,000 you paid a 91% rate. This scaling of tax liability is based on a straightforward, if highly contentious principle. The more you earn, the larger portion of those earnings should go toward the general funding of government and greater good of society. What is tendered in taxes is apportioned by ability to pay.

Granted, the above chart represents an extreme example of progressive taxation in our history. But it was very typical for almost two decades. The 91% rate was in effect 1946-1951 and 1954-1963. It was only exceeded at the end of WWII, 1944-1945 (94%) and two years in the 50s, 1952-1953 (92%).

Obviously, this inspired a lot of odium among the wealthy. They claimed such a contrivance is intrinsically flawed. Because we are all just individuals, one person equal to every other in the eyes of God, we all should receive equal treatment. Just because some individuals are cleverer or financially better off than others should not single them out to be penalized or punished. Conservatives insist that tax rates should therefore be regressive – no fancy formulas and sliding scales – as opposed to progressive. We currently have a progressive tax schedule, though not as drastic as in 1944-1963. The range is 10% to a maximum of 37%.

The most radically *regressive* counter to progressive taxation schedules proposed by extreme conservatives is the flat tax. We merely calculate how much money is needed and based on that, derive a single percentage, a tax rate applied across the board equally to everyone.

While it is elegantly simple and seems to smack of common sense, let's do a simple thought experiment to see how it would play out in the real world.

For our example, let's use a fairly modest flat tax rate of 30%.

Current HHS Poverty Guidelines state that for the 48 contiguous states and District of Columbia, the poverty threshold for a family of four is $30,000. Such a family unit would be required to pay $9,000 in federal taxes, leaving them $21,000 to cover all family living expenses for the year. That would be housing, food, transportation, clothing, utilities, health care, etc. All the necessities for basic subsistence for four people on $21,000. The brutal truth is they would be confronted with a choice between eating and having a roof over their heads. The average rent for the 48 contiguous states and District of Columbia is $1,095 per month. There goes $13,140 for the year. That leaves $5.38 per day to feed each member of the family. I guess if they ate dog food, they could survive. Of course, there would be no money for anything else.

Mind you, the figures just quoted are regarded by many credible COL sites as ridiculously conservative. One says a family of four needs $70,784 to survive. Another one puts it at $92,989, more than three times the poverty line figure we used as an example.

Moving on.

Jeff Bezos' "annual earnings" is hard to nail down. It's definitely a lot of money and one site claims it's $64 billion. At the same time, he sometimes manages to pay little or no taxes. Considering how convoluted his personal finances are, capturing what his "taxable income" might be is like trying to grab grasshoppers in a field at night, blindfolded, using tweezers. For our purposes here, we'll say the 30% flat tax applies to the whole $64 billion, which comes to $19,200,000,000. Brace yourselves and get out the tissues. I'm fighting my own tears as I report this. This means poor Mr. Bezos would be forced to eke out something resembling a decent life for the year on a mere $44,800,000,000. Of course, if he came up short, he could tap into his $161 billion of personal wealth. You know, to make the credit card payments on time and keep gas in the tank. Incidentally, as an aside, spending a million dollars a day, it would take over 440 years to spend Bezos' fortune. How long would it take that family of four to go through the after-flat tax $21,000? Three months?

The obvious point is that debates on political philosophy are non-starters in the real world. Arguing over whether Jeff Bezos deserves to be so rich or not, or whether the Ten Commandments of neoliberal capitalism demand that the ultra-wealthy be handled with kid gloves when it comes to paying taxes, whether grotesque levels of wealth inequality are acceptable, is simply absurd. None of this plays in the real world. We have a country to run and lives to live. We have a nation to cohere and a large complex, highly diverse society to manage and nurture. Divided we fall. Fragmented we fail. The greater good may require the lesser good to be dragged kicking and screaming to embrace compromises which have the greater consensus. Who was it who said "democracy is messy"? The divine right of kings didn't survive modern societal evolution. What place does the divine right of the rich have in a modern functioning democratic nation? I'm not being facetious. Do we have to enforce sensible, constructive tax policy with a guillotine?

By the way, there's method to my madness here.

I'm focusing here on tax policy and its real-world outcomes, because I think that's the perfect vehicle for contrasting our nation's two major political religions: liberal vs. conservative. While recent dramatic shifts on a host of specific issues have caused some confusion as to what these terms precisely mean, they're still useful in identifying the two main political tribes in the U.S. As they too often say, follow the money. The antithetical ways conservatives and liberals approach tax policy pretty much sums up their respective views on the proper relationship between government and the governed.

Having said that, I have no intention of attempting to arbitrate the opposing dogmas of sociopathic conservatism and bleeding-heart liberalism. Each is supported by meticulously cherry-picked facts and impeccable illogic. The simple, straightforward truth is that since these antagonistic positions are generated by completely different, totally incompatible premises and mutually exclusive world views, they inevitably arrive at very different places. There is no way to resolve the differences. However, as I hope you'll discover by the end of this book, that is not to suggest that we as a society must remain mired in confrontation and paralyzed by gridlock.

Back to reality.

I've been citing "official" numbers in terms of what people are supposed to contribute in taxes. The vast majority of everyday citizens play by the book. The wealthy, despite their sanctimonious virtue signaling and interminable whining about onerous tax burdens, do not.

With armies of tax consultants and tax code attorneys at their disposal, the rich don't pay anything close to the official rate. Just look at these four paragons of the neoliberal profit-over-people paradigm.

		Wealth Growth	Total Income Reported		Total Taxes Paid	True Tax Rate
	Warren Buffett *Berkshire Hathaway Inc.*	$24.3B	$125M		$23.7M	**0.10%**
	Jeff Bezos *Amazon.com Inc.*	$99.0B	$4.22B		$973M	**0.98%**
	Michael Bloomberg *Bloomberg LP*	$22.5B	$10.0B		$292M	**1.30%**
	Elon Musk *Tesla Inc.*	$13.9B	$1.52B		$455M	**3.27%**

The agenda of the super-wealthy is not at all opaque or complicated. They want to keep as much money as they can by paying as little in taxes as possible. This dramatically and negatively impacts all of us. To keep their overall tax burden down, they aggressively cut spending. The list is chilling: Medicare for veterans; funding for schools with low-income students and students with disabilities; funding for pre-school and childcare; meager allocations for WIC, i.e. nutrition assistance for women, infants and children; funding for Meals on Wheels which provides nutrition services for seniors; housing choice vouchers for seniors and veterans; funding for NIH, which means delays in cancer and Alzheimer's research. Still high on the Republican agenda is the longstanding goal of cutting Social Security and Medicare.

Taking a sledgehammer to initiatives which offer comfort, relief and support, often to the most vulnerable and disadvantaged, appears to liberals as cruel, selfish, inhumane, unconscionable, vicious and diabolically insensitive. Yet – and it pains me to say this – it's important to acknowledge that for conservatives, it's none of the above. For them it's merely being prudent and responsible, only paying for what we can afford. They insist we simply don't have the money to take care of everyone in need. Of course, conservatives install a big, fat monkey wrench in the machinery. Relentlessly insisting on tax decreases *guarantees* we're always short on money. And the con doesn't stop there. Their relentless calls to cut taxes is then given further justification. We're told that letting the "job creators" keep more of their personal wealth and corporate profits is great for the economy. And a thriving economy eliminates the need for all those expensive social programs. Thus, the less the wealthy pay in taxes, the better off we all are. So the argument goes.

Quite a web of magical thinking being floated, for sure.

At the same time, it is powerful, persuasive magical thinking, propagated by well-funded think tanks, promoted by influential economists, reinforced constantly by toadying pundits and the wholly captured media. Understand, this assault on the common good has been underway for over five decades. The focus and hard work of this blitz shows. The wealthy have perfected their game, while the defenders of us everyday citizens have been left scrambling, often bickering among themselves like alley cats, thrown into disarray by getting pointlessly sidetracked – identity politics, though valid and important, is a perfect example of such squandering of energy and time – thus rendered incapable of formulating and agreeing on a coherent alternative vision, based on fairness and respect for the general welfare and common good. Or as with the Democratic Party, would-be reformers have simply been bought out.

We need a fresh start. We need to look at our situation with fresh eyes.

This is where the candidacy of Robert F. Kennedy Jr. comes in. He is asking the right questions, the tough questions, the necessary questions.

What kind of country do we want to live in and what do we need to do to make that happen? In a true democracy, the 'we' runs the show. Everyone has to give, as well as take. Everyone has to make sacrifices. Everyone has to think in terms of the "everyone".

Timeless inspiration helps.

> "Ask not what your country can do for you. Ask what you can do
> for your country." – John F. Kennedy, January 20, 1961

This is a very tall order, both profound and fragile. Yet, it sounds as fresh and relevant today as it did sixty plus years ago when it was first spoken.

Now we are presented again with an opportunity to meet that challenge.

RFK Jr's message couldn't be more timely or critical for our future. The posturing by both major parties is a deadly pas de deux that's impoverishing everyday citizens, vanquishing the middle class, destroying the American dream, and further bloating the vast fortunes of the wealthy. It's easy to blame just the Republicans for this, but Mr. Kennedy has been reaching out to both sides – Republicans and Democrats – in a call for unity and a promise of hope.

I only hope his enemies – the enemies of "the people" – are paralyzed and incapable of torpedoing what may be our last chance to save America.

R is for regressive.

R is for rapacious.

R is for ruthless.

The Devolution of the Republican Party
From this . . .
. . . to THIS!

What Kind of America Do We Want?

What kind of America do most Americans want?

It's hardly a secret.

The truth is, it's incredibly easy to answer this basic question.

Here, issue-by-issue, are the results of some very recent, credible polls.

74% of Americans want a federal minimum wage of $20.00 per hour.

86% of voters want fair trade agreements protecting jobs, workers, the environment.

61% of voters want a cut back on military spending.

88% of voters want no reductions in Social Security; 82% of voters support expanding it.

69% of voters want Medicare for All.

80% of voters oppose the "Citizens United" U.S. Supreme Court decision.

67% of voters think taxes on the wealthy should be increased.

69% of voters think corporations should be required to pay their fair share in taxes.

83% of voters support massive infrastructure repair, renewal and upgrading.

65% of voters want laws to combat climate change.

69% of voters want tuition free at public colleges and universities.

84% of voters believe valid photo ID should be required to vote. 63% of voters want the president elected by popular vote. 71% of voters want early voting to be made easier. 75% of voters want early voting to be held for two weeks. 74% of voters want election day to be an official legal holiday. 65% of voters support same day voter registration.

Okay, time for a … *pop quiz!*

I know how incredibly smart anyone reading this book must be.

I'm not doing this to be cute.

I'll be asking a serious and revealing question.

By the way, you can use your smart phones or tablets, Google or Bing or Duck Duck Go. You can go to the library or consult your psychic advisor. I want everyone to look good here.

So … here's the question:

What do every one of the above proposals have in common?

(I don't think you'll be pleased with the correct answer.)
Tick ... tick ... tick ...tick.
Times up. Let's see how you did.
What all of these initiatives have in common, despite the fact that year after year, similar polls of public opinion come up with the same results is ...

NONE OF THEM EVER GETS DONE!

Congress meets on average for 182 days out of every year, accumulating collectively thousands of hours of meetings, debates, speeches, roll calls, press conferences, on and on. But they never get around to doing what is expected of them. What is in demand by the majority of U.S. citizens.

The biggest insult is that many of the individuals running for Congress in election after election *offer memes, slogans, sound bites, and even explicit promises* which would lead any sensible, credulous voter to think that they really, truly, honestly are committed to serving the people, that is, going to Washington DC and doing the job they're elected to do. Then these same individuals, now with the election under their belts disappear inside the DC bubble and vote as their deep-pocketed campaign donors, i.e. their ruling elite puppet masters, want them to vote.

This in a nutshell is why the rich get richer, the powerful yield more power, our elected officials keep flying high, while the rest of us are hurting, the worst-off scraping bottom.

This is not democracy. This is fraud.

What kind of America do we want?

I don't think I'm going out on a limb here: We the people, the common citizens who don't have chauffeurs, offshore accounts, investment portfolios stuffed with defense contractor stocks and commodities derivatives, we everyday folks who work for a living and dream of safe streets, good schools, clean air and water ... *we want an America that works for everyone!*

Congress vs. The President

Understanding what has sabotaged our democracy, looking objectively at the way things now work, is the first important step toward restoring things to how they should work.

To get a handle on this, sometimes we need to review the basics.

Granted, there has been an ascendancy over the past few decades of what is called the "imperial presidency". Two mutually reinforcing developments account for this. Congress itself has become timid, less assertive, at times simply complacent. It is rewarded for making a lot of noise but laying low and often being inert. It's more than happy to gutlessly cede its responsibilities in order to avoid blame for the negative impact of tough decisions. The most profound example of this was the Federal Reserve Act passed in December 1913, totally turning over to private banking institutions the authority to issue currency. A more recent example is the 2001 Authorization for Use of Military Force (AUMF), a joint resolution by Congress in response to the 9/11 terrorist attacks, which turned over its constitutional responsibility of declaring and waging war, to George W. Bush. This short, very broad statement was used by three presidents to conduct 37 military operations in 15 countries, without once consulting Congress.

On the other hand, reinforcing this congressional unassertiveness, we find presidents who in sharp contrast, are extremely aggressive in exercising their power. Signing statements to bills passed by Congress is one example, which is often a president saying, "I'll sign this but I object to these specific clauses." Congress and the public have been put on notice: Don't expect these items to be rigorously enforced. They may be ignored altogether.

Then there is, of course, the twisting of existing laws and regulations. White House lawyers get together and write some convoluted legalese to take existing legislation and extend it far beyond its original intent, making possible by manipulation and sometimes surreal "reinterpretation" all sorts of presidential and executive branch misbehavior. A famous and certainly appalling example of this was John Yoo and team's Torture Memos of 2002, used as the legal basis by the Bush administration for setting policy on horrifying detention practices and cruel prisoner abuse.

Most abused of all are executive orders. These are policy dictates being used more and more frequently by "imperial presidents" to circumnavigate Congress into all sorts of questionable realms. The handling of the Covid-19 crisis offers an abundance of examples of this: the shutdowns, lockdowns, mandates, etc. Did any of us have a say in any of this? Was there even a single public or congressional debate? Nothing. Just orders decreed from above.

Such presidential overreach flies in the face of the distribution of power defined in the Constitution. And a veto-proof Congress – 2/3rds majorities in both the House and Senate – which objects to what a president does, has more than enough power to slap down and reverse abuse of executive privilege. It can defund such activities, i.e. cut off the money. It can pass legislation anytime reversing any actions by the president which are not specifically authorized in law by Congress.

The point here is simple: A president can lead but that doesn't guarantee that Congress will follow.

And please remember: This cuts both ways. A rotten president can be immobilized by an enlightened Congress which puts its foot down and stands its ground. Or a president trying to do magnificent things can be kneecapped by the kind of Congress we now have. This is fundamental to our system of "checks and balances". It doesn't necessarily guarantee good outcomes. That entirely depends on us … we the people exercising responsible voting.

The distribution of power, whether autocratically inclined presidents like it or not, is summed up in two truisms:

Congress can impeach the President.

But the President cannot impeach Congress.

It is perhaps convenient, perhaps comforting, to think that electing the "right man or woman" to the presidency assures bold action and big changes. But that's less than half of the story. As I already pointed out, a strong, determined president can lead, but that's no guarantee that the folks on Capitol Hill will follow. This is obvious if you've been paying any attention over the past decades. The fact that people seem to forget just how constrained a president really is, I believe, stems mostly the way the media handles reporting of elections. The preferred narratives focus on personalities and drama, particularly the head-to-head clashes of those aspiring to the highest office in the land. Everything else gets short shrift. There is no balanced and nuanced discussion of issues, the way government constitutionally is designed to operate, the realities of the power struggle between the three branches. This, coupled with obsessing over and reducing every dispute over vital issues to a Democrat vs. Republican cock fight, creates a toxic atmosphere which guarantees a failure to constructively resolve disputes, and makes serious, intelligent, balanced, discussion of critical matters impossible. The public only ends up divided, angered, predictably confused, ill-informed, ill-prepared, and totally ill-equipped to make sense out of anything going on in Washington DC.

Yes, we need the right person in the White House.

But understand that lacking the right people in Congress that president is helpless and largely irrelevant.

We need both.

Urgently!

435 House Seats

As with every federal election, there are 435 House of Representatives seats up for grabs in 2024. If history repeats itself, most of those will be filled by incumbents, those currently holding office.

Now I'm going to really go out on a limb here and say something so extreme, you won't know whether to laugh or try to get a refund for this book.

Here it is …

NONE of those currently filling those 435 House seats, most of whom will run for reelection are fit for office. NONE OF THEM!

Proving this is honestly very simple.

Refer back to the chapter "What Kind of America Do We Want?"

Based on that I'm going to propose a simple, straightforward test for you to determine if your current congressman or congresswoman deserves such a cushy, well-paid job, sitting in the power center of our nation – some would contend, the center of the Universe – respected and revered, with lobbyists and pundits alike swarming at their feet like groupies.

IS YOUR CONGRESSIONAL REPRESENTATIVE
QUALIFIED TO REPRESENT YOU?

1) Did your current representative *ever* introduce a bill in Congress to raise the minimum wage to $20.00 per hour? How about $15.00 per hour?

2) Did your current representative *ever* introduce a bill in Congress to institute fair trade agreements? Protection for domestic jobs? Safeguarding the environment?

3) Did your current representative *ever* introduce a bill or vote in support of decreasing the military budget?

4) Did your current representative *ever* introduce a bill in Congress to protect Social Security? To raise the tax cap on Social Security to keep it solvent?

5) Did your current representative *ever* introduce a bill in Congress to institute Medicare for All? How about any legislation guaranteeing affordable, quality health care for every single U.S. citizen?

6) Did your current representative *ever* introduce a bill in Congress to reverse the Citizens United decision?

7) Did your current representative *ever* introduce a bill in Congress to fix the rapidly crumbling infrastructure of our country?

8) Did your current representative *ever* introduce a bill in Congress reforming tax law so that the wealthy and corporations pay their fair share?

9) Did your current representative *ever* introduce a bill in Congress to address climate change? Even a token bill recommending the country try to live sustainably?

10) Did your current representative *ever* introduce a bill in Congress to make tuition free at public colleges and universities?

11) Did your current representative *ever* introduce a bill in Congress to attempt to fix our disastrous electoral system? Make it easier to vote?

Already, I can hear one objection loud and clear: *'ever* <u>introduce</u> a bill in Congress'? That's certainly a tall order. Getting a bill up for consideration is a BIG DEAL.

Exactly! It is a big deal. It's a lot of hard work, involves a lot of research, countless hours of nudging and cajoling to muster support.

But since it's such a *big deal*, it says something about a congressperson. It says they're serious, truly committed, willing to fight for their constituents.

What? You would prefer someone who sits around waiting for another representative to do the hard work? This is exactly why as I said at the end of the "What Kind of America Do We Want?" chapter, nothing ever gets done. Too many mediocre, lazy, insulated, indifferent phonies, puffed up on their importance, parked in the big domed building, who are not intent on truly representing THE PEOPLE. I'm guessing your congressman is one of them.

But wait! I'm not quite finished. I have one more test item.

Early in August 2023, CNN conducted a poll. Support for the Ukraine military is quickly waning. "Most Americans oppose Congress authorizing additional funding to support Ukraine in its war with Russia, according to a new CNN poll conducted by SSRS, as the public splits over whether the US has already done enough to assist Ukraine. Overall, 55% say the US Congress should not authorize additional funding to support Ukraine vs. 45% who say Congress should authorize such funding."

Now let me venture a guess here, one that has 100% certainty. That is, by the time this book is published, those percentages will be 80% to 20%. Because by then, Ukraine will be defeated, and people will finally figure out that this whole rah-rah Ukraine business has been a LIE OF BIBLICAL PROPORTIONS! That the death and destruction in Ukraine is an insidious, cruel joke. That we've completely wasted over $130 billion, which we needed back here in the U.S. for a myriad of reasons. And the most insulting, treacherous, nauseating discovery of all: That there was no reason why the conflict between US/NATO/Ukraine and Russia ever had to happen. The war was completely unnecessary.

Which is what Robert F. Kennedy, Jr. has been saying all along!

So here, folks, is the final item for determining if your congressperson is qualified to serve …

> 12) Did your current representative vote to fund the fiasco
>   in Ukraine? Did he or she even ask obvious questions
>   about the wisdom of promoting this nightmare?

If the answers to any 5 of the questions 1–11 are 'NO' and/or the answer to question 12 is 'YES', your congressman or congresswoman should be given an electoral pink slip, sent packing, *unelected* – no explanation needed!

Why am I being so harsh? So drastic? So extreme?

Look at the percentages listed in the earlier "What Kind of America Do We Want?" chapter. People know what needs to get done. And it never does. We hear excuses, empty rhetoric, vacant promises. We should be mad as hell! But more important than being mad as hell is doing something about it.

Representing the needs and desires of those who charge a person with the responsibility to do just that, is one of the most important jobs in our nation. It is the essence of democracy, government of the people, by the people, for the people. Our elected officials *work for us! ... answer to us! ... report to us!*

At least they're supposed to. Recognize, when the essential relationship between citizen and their chosen representatives breaks down – when elected officials ignore the "job description" outlined in the Constitution – that's the end of democracy. Period! We end up with what we now have: a Congress of play-for-pay lapdogs to the ruling elite [https://bit.ly/3raS71p].

As to funding the Ukrainian war, the decision for military intervention on such a massive scale as we see in Ukraine, is monumental, perhaps the most consequential decision a government official can make. Tens of thousands of lives are at stake, both soldiers and civilians. It's not to be taken lightly.

Did anyone in Congress – ANYONE? – ask any tough questions about Ukraine? Did anyone do some research into the history of the conflict, which in truth didn't start on February 24th of 2022 when Russia sent in their troops, but went all the way back to 2014? The persecution of ethnic Russians living in Donbas started then. 14,000 people dead *before* Russia's recent intervention.

What about Russia's repeated attempts to avoid military confrontation? Did anyone in Congress talk about the Minsk II Agreement? Or the draft treaties proposed by Russia in December 2021, which precluded the need for this horrible military conflict?

Does anyone in Congress even know about any of this? How is it a misfit like me, living in Japan in the middle of rice and soybean fields, can find all the necessary background information and know the truth about Ukraine, and these very well-positioned, well-connected powerful government officials, with the best researchers in the nation available to them, with access to vast amounts of data and analysis from the intel agencies, haven't got a clue? Do our elected representatives just watch CNN and Fox News and call it a day?

Did anyone in Congress take a moment and question why they were being stampeded like dumb cattle into this war? Where was AOC? What about the "squad"? They're supposedly progressives. Don't progressives believe in peace anymore?

Perhaps even more incriminating in terms of the values the U.S. loudly trumpets to the rest of the world, did everyone in Congress forget the words 'peace' and 'diplomacy'? How is starting and perpetuating senseless slaughter consistent with the U.S. claim to be spreading democracy, justice, freedom, and human rights? What about the right for people and their families to not be blown to smithereens in their homes or walking down the street? What about the right to not have your streets, playgrounds, fields and farmlands be strewn with unexploded cluster bombs for the next five decades? Or cancer-causing depleted uranium?

The truth is, almost the entire Congress to the last person, was derelict in their duty. They lined up like dimwitted lemmings and raised no serious objections to throwing away $130 billion. While America has over 550,000 homeless people. While 40 million people go to bed hungry at night. While 30 million still don't have health insurance. While inflation is making many choose between feeding their families and heating their homes. SHAMEFUL!

So yes, I expect some tough questions and critical thinking, some serious research and probing from our legislators. Why should we support this war? What American interests are served by fueling a conflict thousands of miles from our shores with tens of billions of dollars? If these legislators are too lazy or too stupid to do their jobs, then what other conclusion can we draw? They are unfit for office and should be replaced.

Having said that, and being a generous, open-minded, all-around decent person, let me offer incumbents – as well as new candidates for legislative office – an opportunity to prove themselves. That is, if they can offer absolute proof that now they see the light, offering an ironclad guarantee they are on the path of the straight and true, that they fully understand their responsibility to the voting public, will serve with zeal, loyalty, integrity, honesty, transparency, humility, and unwavering dedication their constituents – those who invest their faith in them by voting them into office – then both the repentant, reformed incumbents and new candidates for congressional positions, should be looked at objectively and regarded as a viable choice.

Such an ironclad guarantee does exist. What it looks like will be covered in a subsequent chapter: "The Kennedy Candidate Voter Contract".

34 Senate Seats

Here are the Senate seats that will be contested November 2024, and who now fills them:

State:	Current Senator:	Terms Served:	2024 Status:
AZ	Kyrsten Sinema (I)	1	Running
CA	Dianne Feinstein (D)	6	Not Running
CT	Chris Murphy (D)	2	Running
DE	Tom Carper (D)	4	Not Running
FL	Rick Scott (R)	1	Running
HI	Mazie Hirono (D)	2	Running
IN	Mike Braun (R)	1	Not Running
MA	Elizabeth Warren (D)	2	Running
MD	Ben Cardin (D)	3	Not Running
ME	Angus King (I)	2	Running
MI	Debbie Stabenow (D)	4	Not Running
MN	Amy Klobuchar (D)	3	Running
MO	Josh Hawley (R)	1	Running
MS	Roger Wicker (R)	3	Running
MT	Jon Tester (D)	3	Running
ND	Kevin Cramer (R)	1	Running
NE	Deb Fischer (R)	2	Running
NE	Pete Ricketts (R)	1	Running
NJ	Bob Menendez (D)	4	Running
NM	Martin Heinrich (D)	2	Running
NV	Jacky Rosen (D)	1	Running
NY	Kirsten Gillibrand (D)	3	Running
OH	Sherrod Brown (D)	3	Running
PA	Bob Casey (D)	3	Running
RI	Sheldon Whitehouse (D)	3	Running
TN	Marsha Blackburn (R)	1	Running
TX	Ted Cruz (R)	2	Running
UT	Mitt Romney (R)	1	Running
VA	Tim Kaine (D)	2	Running
VT	Bernie Sanders (I)	4	Running
WA	Maria Cantwell (D)	4	Running
WI	Tammy Baldwin (D)	2	Running
WV	Joe Manchin (D)	3	Running
WY	John Barrasso (R)	3	Running

We have five current senators not seeking reelection, and twenty-nine incumbents looking for another 6-year term.

Everything said in the previous chapter applies to these senatorial races. Incumbents looking for another win make it very easy to determine if they're worthy. We have at minimum a voting record of six years of legislation to look at, to determine if they made a credible attempt at serving the people. Nine incumbents have been in office for twelve years, ten for eighteen years. Five have been fixtures in the Senate Chamber for twenty-four years! All of these senators have had plenty of time to prove themselves. Did they introduce bills for the eleven initiatives which are hugely important to the public or not? Did they vote in recent sessions to fund the nightmare still unfolding in Ukraine?

This is not difficult work. We have the internet. Nor is it rocket science.

Frankly, it's pretty straightforward. Either these elected officials are genuinely on the side of the people or they're not.

Almost all politicians sound alike, are master level actors, offering lovely words and promises which play on the credulity and patronize the desires of the voting public. We must ignore their words and look only at their actions. That's where we'll find either loyalty or treachery. For any incumbent to *earn* our trust and *warrant* our support in the voting booth, they need to PROVE TO US they are deserving, they are trustworthy, they are dependable, they are what we are looking for to unwaveringly, without caveat or qualification, represent our interests, priorities and values when they arrive in our nation's capital.

The same criteria, of course, apply to newcomers. Without being able to reference a voting record, we must depend exclusively on a different device. This will be fully explained thoroughly in a later chapter: "The Kennedy Candidate Voter Contract".

The point is, we as citizens, as voters, as guardians and enablers of our future, must not let emotions get in our way. We should apply objectively, fairly, and dispassionately the recommended tests, to determine if a candidate, an incumbent or a newcomer, is qualified for office.

We owe it to ourselves to root out the corruption of our system, to rid ourselves of those individuals who have been gaming the electoral process and violating the basic terms of our Constitution in service to a powerful elite, to introduce true representative democracy by only sending to Washington DC elected officials who will work for us, report to us, answer to us.

We can do this.

Regime Change in Washington DC

Regime change?

Isn't that a bit extreme?

Not really. What is extreme is believing against all available evidence that the politicos "representing us" actually represent us. *That* is extremely ridiculous. What is extreme is thinking that if we just appeal to these power puppets, sign some petitions, write some letters, have some Zoom meetings, let them know we're not happy with the state of our country, explain in clear logical terms why it's important to get done the things we want done, a big lightbulb will light up above their heads, common sense will prevail, and they'll magically come around. *That* is extremely delusional.

Refer back to just some of the changes huge majorities of U.S. citizens have been demanding for decades: "What Kind of America Do We Want?"

Again, what do these all have in common?

THEY NEVER GET DONE!

Do you need any more proof that we need to clean house in DC?

I'm not talking about violent regime change.

But it's regime change, nevertheless.

Clean sweep. Start over. Except perhaps for those few incumbents who *guarantee* they'll end their loyalty to the ruling elite, the corporate class, the Deep State, and start serving "we the people" – all of us honest, hardworking folk who built this country!

What does ousting these disloyal, arguably treacherous legislators from office come down to? What is the process?

The official mechanisms available to get "good guy" candidates on the ballot are rigged in favor of establishment, centrist lapdogs to the oligarchs – the rich and powerful who now run things – making it a very challenging task.

But it can be done. And how it will be done is emblematic and exemplary.

We are looking at grassroots democracy in the purest sense: citizens working together outside the "system" but using the system to its advantage. Citizens getting together by their own initiative, organized as they wish and themselves determine, making important decisions at the community level, bottom-up, embracing the policies which work for them as everyday citizens, to improve their lives and the quality of life in their homes and neighborhoods.

Maybe this will seem naïve. I hope not. Sometimes the shortest distance is a straight line, the best strategy simple and straightforward.

How do you replace your non-performing, tone-deaf congressperson?

It begins by finding a replacement. An *amazing* replacement!

We clearly don't need more of the same, i.e. self-serving, self-promoting "career politicians" we've had. We need someone who will SERVE the public and directly attend to the greater good of the country. Someone who listens and takes his or her marching orders from the good, decent folks who vote them into office. Someone who has the focus, confidence, integrity, strength of will, to go to Washington DC and do the job they're elected to do. Not kowtow to special interests, lobbyists, wealth campaign donors, but work 24/7 to improve the lives of all U.S. citizens. This would include huge increases in wages, a health care system that delivers the best health care in the world to 100% of the citizenry, secure borders, affordable quality education, good jobs, safe streets, clean air and water, healthy nutritious food, respect for privacy, freedom from illegal surveillance by the security agencies, free and open media, an internet that's universally accessible and free from censorship, modern infrastructure, efficient transportation systems, an end to endless wars and a bloated military. That's just a short list.

We begin by looking in our local communities. If the polls are correct, finding individuals who are aware of the problems and want effective solutions should be easy. The real challenge is finding someone who 1) we trust, 2) is electable, and 3) is willing to endure the cage fight political campaigns have become.

What would that person look like?

He or she might be an educator, a teacher, principal or professor. Maybe a minister or someone active in charity work in the community. He or she might be a town or city councilman, a former mayor, a police chief or a fire marshal. Even a respected businessperson, someone who is known to be fair, generous and honest. He or she might not have ever held elected office but been an active participant in community organizations, involved with helping disadvantaged and at-risk youth, instrumental in arranging care for the elderly. He or she might be a prominent and highly regarded member of an NPO or NGO, an environmentalist, advocate for the homeless, head of a pet rescue and animal shelter. He or she might be that person who is always at town hall and city board meetings, outspoken and full of creative ideas to improve the condition of the local city or town, and the safety and comfort of its citizens.

They're out there. And they don't have to have a political science degree from Princeton or a law degree from Harvard. They don't even need prior experience as a public office holder or even working in government.

If the track record of our current crop of political professionals says anything, it could be argued that it might be viewed as a *liability* to have held an elected position before. I'm not being snarky. The best argument for term limits is looking at how incumbents increasingly fail to perform as they are repeatedly reelected. It would appear that they get way too comfortable inside that Washington DC bubble and start taking their constituents for granted. So experience does not necessarily equate to competence and devoted service.

Finland offers an exemplary model for encouraging citizen participation. Over five decades, it has initiated a number of sweeping reforms to ensure that everyday people are actively involved at all levels of government, providing a host of different channels, to participate in making the decisions which shape policy and create the social/political/economic environment for a free, open, prosperous, comfortable, stable society. There are no restrictions on age, social status, income, level of education. All opinions and views are welcome.

> "The legally mandated right of participation has developed and evolved rapidly since the 1970s in Finland. Since the 1990s, these changes have picked up pace and opportunities for direct participation have been added to the traditional focus on representative democracy. Finland's commitment to civic participation, as part of its commitment to democracy more generally, extends from its Constitution to legislation, policy and practice, from the central government across the ministries and right down to the municipal level. It is underpinned by a strong commitment to transparency and openness and facilitated by high levels of trust in governance institutions."

By the way, this includes running for office in Finland. This assures that the voice of regular people is heard loud and clear, the only way possible for democracy and self-government to maintain integrity and robustness.

Now, this may appear to be a rather harsh assessment, but it seems that in America the opposite is true. It's put up and shut up. *That* has got to change. We must encourage and support anyone who has something of value to contribute to the national conversation. Moreover, we must identify those individuals – the future leaders for a renewed America, a truly democratic America – who reflect the values, interests, and priorities of all the citizenry, individuals who are trustworthy, articulate, focused, and determined, then take them all the way to the top, working for we the people in our nation's capital.

Let me say that I find it inconceivable that in a country of more than 340 million people, we can't identify 469 individuals who fit the above description. Individuals with the right values, the integrity, the willingness to serve their country in a profound and meaningful way. Impossible! I don't know very many people, but I guarantee you among my acquaintances, there are 20-25 such persons. It's just a matter of getting out in the community, looking around, talking to others. Despite its behavior on the international stage, despite the horrifying example set by the people now in power, America is and has always been a country of good, decent individuals. So that person you're looking for to challenge your current smile-and-do-nothing puppet-to-the-ruling-elite congressperson, is out there. The person who will bring the required intelligence, commitment, honesty, loyalty, and service to the job of representing YOU, is out there.

Get to work!

Grassroots = True Democracy

Who can doubt it? The Kennedy name is legendary! Epic! Monumental! The contributions of this revered family are carved into the history books and ineradicably woven into the fabric of American life.

Now, I don't want to be the bearer of bad news about how that has recently changed. In point of fact, I don't have to be. Because seeing how RFK Jr – the latest Kennedy in public life – is being portrayed by the reactionary enemies of progress and reform, is as easy as turning on a TV, glancing at a smart phone, or visiting any legacy media site. If you can handle it, just look at RFK Jr's Wikipedia page, which is one, long slanderous smear job from top to bottom. According to that Deep State-rigged website, he's an anti-science kook peddling dangerous and simple-minded conspiracy theories.

How do these purveyors of slime reconcile the new "demon Kennedy" with the legendary reputation of the Kennedy brand? Here's an educated guess: *Those other Kennedys were great. But you know every family has one. A black sheep, a bad apple, a nutcase in the attic.* To support this skewed appraisal, I've seen a lot of mention by talking heads of how the rest of the Kennedy family hates RFK Jr, how they shun him, think his ideas are loony.

Fiendish endless-war/Deep-State/MIC/Wall-Street/investment-bank inner circles are notably behind much of the slander and vilification. They most definitely don't want RFK Jr in the White House. After all, he keeps talking about ending the war in Ukraine, working with Russia and China to have peaceful competition and cooperation. There goes the bloated DOD budgets and gravy train for military industries and war profiteers. 'Peace' is the foulest of foul expletives to these sociopathic predators.

Other heavy-weight industry sector influencers oppose him as well. He's talking about eliminating regulatory agency capture, meaning industries will have to start playing by the rules and obeying regulations intended to keep the public safe. He'll end the unwarranted cash cow subsidies to already highly profitable businesses. And then there's the unthinkable! RFK Jr just might – horror of horrors! – demand that both corporations and high-rollers start paying their fair share in taxes. All of which says, for the establishment ruling elite, stopping RFK Jr or anyone like him from exposing their deceit and wholesale plunder of the economy, especially from the highest office in the land, is a matter of life or death. The ugly, appalling truth is that these self-serving psychos would really prefer having a senile mannikin or a token-minority woken bimbo lead the country, someone they could totally control. Someone who keeps the public confused, disoriented, divided, paralyzed. Does that explain why we currently have what we have in the White House?

Safety tip: Don't underestimate the rich and powerful. They feel deeply threatened by Robert F. Kennedy Jr and are ruthless to the core. Malicious attacks on his character are just the opening salvo. To be blunt about it, I fear the worst. And Joe Biden won't give him Secret Service protection. That right there says a lot, eh?

So …

The battle lines have been drawn. As military mastermind Sun Tzu says: Know the enemy. Know the enemy better than the enemy knows himself.

And just as critically, we must recognize how formidable this challenge is and how limited our own resources are. The establishment controls the media, the government, the police, the military, and at least for now, Congress.

Truthfully, there's only one way to fight this: That is to relentlessly counter the ad hominem attacks and disinformation with the truth. Get out there and enlighten people. Demonstrate beyond a shadow of a doubt that the lies about RFK Jr and his agenda do not hold up to the reality of the man. Show them the real Robert F. Kennedy, Jr. and what he stands for. What kind of America he envisions. What he will do to make that America a reality.

This isn't possible using official established channels of communication. Establishment news media is the enemy. Moreover, social media is censored, controlled, its effectiveness fatally compromised for individuals speaking any truth that doesn't align with the approved narratives. We already know where the Democratic Party stands. It will do everything in its power to delegitimize RFK Jr and make certain his presidential bid doesn't see the light of day. I refer you to Bernie Sanders 2016 for proof.

The only way to get RFK Jr's message to the voting public is to take it directly to the people. State by state, district by district, city by city, town by town, neighborhood by neighborhood … people to people.

This is the foundation of a true democracy. Building consensus with TV ads, rah-rah rallies, bumper stickers and yard signs works. Who can doubt that? But these pale next to personal conversation. Word of mouth. When people talk and hash things out, look at the problems, exchange ideas, weigh different proposals and possible directions, then arrive at a viable set of solutions, *that's* true participatory democracy. When a candidate is identified who embraces those solutions, is deemed trustworthy and capable of introducing and promoting those solutions to become the law of the land, then chosen by popular vote to be that one special individual who goes to Washington DC to work on behalf of the people of that district or state, *that's* true representative democracy. It's as good as it gets under our Constitution.

Robert F. Kennedy, Jr. is a magnificent, powerful, visionary man, the kind of individual who comes along way too infrequently. He deserves our trust, our loyalty, our dedication.

But he's only one man.

And it takes a whole Congress to shape the laws which determine the future of our nation. I certainly hope by now that the main message of this book has sunk in. Yes, we need RFK Jr in the White House. But for him to accomplish anything at all, for our country to get back on track, requires a Kennedy-supportive Congress.

This means that local activism, grassroots organizing for the 2024 election, equates to and requires killing two birds with
one stone. And it must be handled with care
and calculation. I believe that when approaching most voters, instead of talking about the presidential race right from the get-go – a presidential contest which already has huge, ugly battle lines drawn for a Trump-Biden shoot out – initiating a conversation about the House and Senate races is a much more promising opening.

"What's with our congressman? He says one thing but does another."

"Don't they all?"

"Do you know he voted to raise the eligibility age for Social Security? And against Medicare-4-All? How long has he been in office? Eight years?"

"The problem is there's never a good alternative."

"Well, this time there is. Ever heard of Thomas Green? He's running in the primary against that blowhard we now have."

"Wasn't he on the city council? A retired schoolteacher, right?"

"That's the fellow. A really good person. He's a Kennedy Democrat!"

"Kennedy Democrat? What's that?"

"The nephew of John F. Kennedy is running for president. Totally on the side of the people! He is committed to cleaning up government, you know, making it work for everybody, not just the rich and powerful. The idea is to put him in the White House, and at the same time, put people in Congress that are 100% behind him. No more gridlock. A new Congress and President Robert F Kennedy, Jr. working together for us regular folks."

We need to have conversations like this going on all over the country, every day of the week. Word-of-mouth is by far the most powerful form of communication. It's personal, interactive, persuasive. Social media is fine too. But it's not the same. What's the expression? Think globally, act locally. How about: Think nationally, now go talk to your neighbor!

The way the presidential race has been turned into a media circus creates a lot of confusion, anger, disconnect with voters. RFK Jr's throwing his hat into the ring has already stirred a lot of controversy and attracted much ire and malicious personal attacks. Good luck getting people to pay attention to his truly noble and powerful message.

Without a doubt, people want things to get done. They want real change. They want leaders on top who are committed to real solutions.

At the same time, their only tangible connection with Washington DC is through their locally elected representatives. If we can convince them that there are candidates running for House and Senate who are not playing games, not just tossing word salad and spewing empty promises to con people into voting for them, candidates who are committed to a genuinely new direction for the country, including straightforward, honest campaigning, there's some hope that as part of their awakening they'll start paying attention and listening to RFK Jr, and through the sheer power and honesty of his words be equipped to ignore the foul, spiteful propaganda currently being generated to destroy his chances for the White House.

It all starts with people, on the ground, in their communities.

Elect a Kennedy candidate to Congress.

Elect RFK Jr as our next president.

The Kennedy Candidate Voter Contract

As already outlined, we need to search for, identify, then promote a "Kennedy candidate" in each of the congressional races for the upcoming 2024 election: 435 for the House of Representatives and 34 for the Senate.

Then the most immediate and critical challenge is determining who truly is on our side.

I offer here a simple, straightforward device. It is based on RFK Jr's own stated positions, available on his kennedy2024.com website. I believe it to be as reliable and foolproof as anything available to us. This is for the House.

KENNEDY CANDIDATE VOTER CONTRACT

U. S. House of Representatives
___ District, State of _______

I, ___________, if elected to a seat in the U.S. House of Representatives representing the ___ District of the State of _______, hereby commit to sponsor or co-sponsor and vote in favor of legislation for the following:

- **Health Care:** Ending the terrible pandemic of chronic disease, targeting autoimmunity, allergies, diabetes, obesity, addiction, anxiety, and depression. Go beyond making existing modalities available to all, to include low-cost alternative and holistic therapies that have been marginalized in a pharma-dominated system. Move the nation from a sick care system to a wellness society.

- **Economy and Jobs:** Rebuild the industrial infrastructure, ruined by forty years of offshoring and misguided "free trade" schemes. Enact policies that favor small and medium businesses, which are the nation's real job creators and the dynamos of American enterprise. Support labor in reclaiming its fair share of American prosperity. Break up "too-big-to-fail" banks and monopolies. When crisis strikes, bail out the homeowners, debtors, and small business owners instead of the banks.

- **Environment and Agriculture:** Initiate programs for building soil, replenishing groundwater, and detoxifying land, all while producing just as much food utilizing conventional farmers earning a decent livelihood. Incentivize the transition of industry to zero-waste cycles and clean energy sources, and forge agreements with other countries to implement these policies throughout the global supply chain. Protect wild lands from further development, by curbing mining, logging, oil drilling, and suburban sprawl. Make the U.S. a global advocate for rainforest preservation and marine restoration.

- **Reducing Military Budget:** Ending the Ukraine conflict and other undeclared wars. End unnecessary military exploits across the globe, except where absolutely required to protect the safety of American citizens, and to defend the nation from overt, verifiable aggression. End the pursuit of empire and pursue peace instead, as a strong and healthy nation.

- **Government Reform:** Remake public institutions to serve the public. Roll back the secrecy and make government transparent. Protect whistleblowers and prosecute officials who abuse the public trust. Rein in the lobbyists and slam shut the revolving door that shunts people from government agencies to lucrative positions in the companies they were supposed to regulate, and back again. Get money out of politics. Open our institutions to real citizen involvement. Restore integrity to government.

- **Regulatory Agencies:** End regulatory agency capture by the enterprises they are supposed to regulate: the SEC by Wall Street; the EPA and BLM by polluters and extractive industries; the CDC, NIH, and FDA by Big Pharma; USDA by Big Ag; FTC by Big Tech.

- **Race Relations:** Repair the damage caused by centuries of bigotry. Take racial healing seriously through a program of Targeted Community Repair. The operating principle is not guilt for the sins of one's ancestors, but rather compassion. Invoke the authentic desire in all Americans, white and black, liberal and conservative, to improve the condition of our Black and Native brothers and sisters.

- **Currency Reform:** Back the United States dollar with hard assets including Bitcoin and precious metals. T-bills would similarly be backed by hard currency, by gold, silver, platinum or Bitcoin.

- **Civil Liberties:** Protect and restore the fundamental civil liberties, enshrined in the Bill of Rights, that hold the essence of what America can be. Dismantle the censorship-industrial complex, in which Big Tech censors, algorithmically suppresses, deplatforms, and shadowbans, any person or opinion the government asks them to. Institute laws which assure the right to privacy and freedom from unreasonable searches and seizures, and end mass surveillance of American citizens and the abuse of civil asset forfeiture. Guarantee that the Covid-era suspension of the right to assembly, trial by jury, and freedom of worship will never happen again. The same for the right to property.

- **Justice and Policing:** Take special care to ensure the civil liberties of minorities and the poor. End the failed War on Drugs and grant amnesty to nonviolent drug offenders. Shut the school-to-prison pipeline, and transition prisons away from a punishment paradigm to a rehabilitation paradigm. Transform the police by incentivizing them to prevent violence, not make unnecessary arrests. Train police in de-escalation and mediation skills and partner them with neighborhood organizations. End the adversarial relationship between citizens and police by focusing law enforcement on serious crimes, not harassing ordinary people.

I will publicly and on the floor of the House of Representatives actively promote all legislation which exclusively supports these measures. If no other legislator comes forth to propose such individual pieces of legislation, I will create and introduce by my own initiative, within 180 days of taking office, legislative acts for each of the foregoing, to be submitted for consideration by Congress.

I further understand and fully agree to the following: If I violate the above-stated terms of this agreement, I will tender on the 181st day after taking the oath of office for my legislative seat, my unconditional resignation from this elected position. Moreover, within one year of my resignation, I will refund all contributions made by individual donors in support of my candidacy for this office.

I sign and will honor this as a legally binding contract, my ironclad guarantee to serve the citizens of this district, the _____ District of the State of _____________, should they choose me as their elected representative.

I sign this agreement voluntarily and with a full appreciation of all its obligations and responsibilities. I accept and will abide by its terms, with a clear understanding of its requirements and implications.

Signed: _______________________

Date: _________________________

A PDF of this contract is available for download @ https://bit.ly/3Pybbjs.

Contracts are also available for the Senate @ https://bit.ly/487yAj2, and for President @ https://bit.ly/44M1YbB.

It is critical to understand what this contract represents.

It is not an attempt to control "good" candidates. The initiatives in the contract should equate to their values and priorities. They list the things they already want to get done if elected. Meaning there's no pressure on them.

The contract is a device for exposing the smooth-talking establishment candidates for what they are: *All talk and no walk.*

How? Establishment candidates cannot and will not sign this document. If they did, they would lose the support of both their campaign donors and whatever major party they're affiliated with.

The only candidates who can and will sign this are candidates who are genuinely behind these needed changes, who will go to Washington DC and do what is needed to put these measures into law.

The contract draws a line in the sand. Either you stand with the majority of U.S. citizens … or you stand with the rich and powerful, the privileged elite.

This device is the most effective method available for determining if a candidate is on "our side" or just blowing more smoke with slick campaign rhetoric and empty promises.

It is a powerful way for a genuine "people's candidate" to establish a direct bond with his or her future constituents. By making the Kennedy Candidate Voter Contract the centerpiece of a campaign, voters will have no doubt what they can expect if they vote this individual into office. It represents his or her marching orders, directly from the voters to the person they have chosen to represent them. In a sense, it is the purest form of democratic representation.

Should a candidate be afraid to sign such a high-powered commitment?

If a candidate truly stands with the people on these issues, the contract already reflects his or her values and priorities. The contract lists the very things he or she believes in and is among the reasons the candidate is running for office in the first place.

Recognizing that in such a litigious society as the U.S. has become, perhaps there might occasionally be instances of anxiety about signing it.

Let me pose a straightforward question …

Why would a "people's candidate" have any qualms about signing such a defining and powerful instrument? If the candidate is serious about getting elected, the contract is among the most effective ways to dispel any doubts and instill confidence among the voting public. It is a loud declaration of loyalty to his or her fellow citizens, an unambiguous and public testimony, a bold commitment to giving the kind of public service American citizens deserve but have long been lacking.

We are confronted with a difficult reality. Congress now is completely corrupted by money and influence peddling. From all the legal troubles mounting against our current and recent presidents, it's obvious that the White House has also been compromised and become captured by the ruling elite.

This election may be our last chance to put an end to such criminal abuse of power and privilege.

Fortunately, we have in Robert F. Kennedy, Jr. a man who will clean up the Executive Branch.

Now it's up to us to replace our current pay-for-play congressional puppets with truly honest, loyal, hard-working individuals who will be faithful both to their constituents and the Constitution.

We must choose wisely.

The Kennedy Candidate Voter Contract is the way to choose wisely.

Crossroads: A Line in the Sand

Perhaps more than facing a crossroads, we are approaching a cliff.

The threat to our democracy and the survival of our once-great nation has reached historic, terrifying heights.

It's been a very gradual, quite subtle, often invisible process.

But we now are staring into the abyss of a totalitarian police state. The mechanisms for assuring a voice by everyday people in the affairs of running the government, and most importantly, sharing in the vast riches and rewards of being citizens in the wealthiest, most powerful nation in history, are all but disabled. Our "democracy", once an example to the rest of the world, has become a mockery of itself. Confidence in simple, straightforward systems which support "government by the people" – e.g. voter registration, recording and tallying votes – is at an all-time low and plummeting.

How do I sound the alarm without sounding like an alarmist?

How about this? … If it's not too late already, it's now or never, folks!

Here's what's at stake in the 2024 election. It's nothing less than the survival of a recognizable version of America! I'm not exaggerating.

At this stage of the game, it looks like one of these folks will be our next president …

Or … or … (gasp!)

DONALD J. TRUMP!

Now, I have no doubt that if you're reading this book, you are strongly in favor of having Robert F. Kennedy Jr. win the presidential election in 2024. That prompts me to further assume that you're intelligent, aware, informed, thoughtful, and a person of the highest moral standards.

That being the case, what now follows – which happens to be the central message and call to action of this short book – should make total sense.

If RFK Jr is elected in 2024, as a president who reports to the "people", truly puts the welfare of all of our citizens ahead of Wall Street, the big banks, the military-industrial complex, the ruling elite and other powerful special interests, thus serves the needs of the all citizens, not just the wealthy elite, *HE WILL NEED A CONGRESS THAT SUPPORTS AND PROMOTES HIS GAME-CHANGING AGENDA*.

But if one of the "bad guys" wins – as has happened for decades – subjecting our nation to economic plunder, endless war, corporate welfare, pay-to-play politics, divide-and-conquer tyranny, thus cheating everyday citizens out of their fair share of our vast national wealth, we will need a Congress that will stop the decline and keep the worst from happening. We'll need a Congress that will end the looting of our economy, the wanton destruction of the environment, the promotion of forever wars and rampant militarization, the marginalization of everyday citizens, the attack on privacy and our human rights, and the concentration of wealth in the hands of a tiny elite. *WE WILL NEED A CONGRESS THAT EMBRACES THE VALUES AND GAME-CHANGING AGENDA OF RFK, JR*.

Meaning that either way ...

WE NEED A "PEOPLE'S CONGRESS"!

WE NEED <u>A KENNEDY CONGRESS</u>!

We need to elect men and women to our legislature who report to and fully represent the needs and priorities of everyday citizens, not special interests, not corporations, not banks, not Wall Street, not the rich and powerful.

Of course, we want a "good guy" to occupy the White House.

Of course, RFK Jr. would be a cosmic improvement as a leader.

At the same time, keep in mind . . .

THE PRESIDENT IS THE LIGHTNING ROD.

BUT <u>CONGRESS</u> IS THE LIGHTNING!

Congress creates and passes the laws that shape everything about our nation: how we care for our citizens, our freedoms, our responsibilities, our relations with every other country on the planet, how we treat the planet itself, war and peace, our economy, our politics, our infrastructure, our monetary and banking systems, our safety, our legal framework, the implementation of justice, our elections, our health care ... EVERYTHING!

For there to be any progress, for our country to start functioning again, for everyday citizens to again have a voice in shaping the future they want for themselves and future generations, WE MUST ELECT A CONGRESS THAT TRULY REPRESENTS AND SERVES THE PEOPLE!

If you understand and embrace what Robert F. Kennedy Jr. has been saying so far in his campaign, that equates to ELECTING A KENNEDY CONGRESS!

Folks ...

We know what has to be done.

Let's do it!

People Power Is Our Only Hope

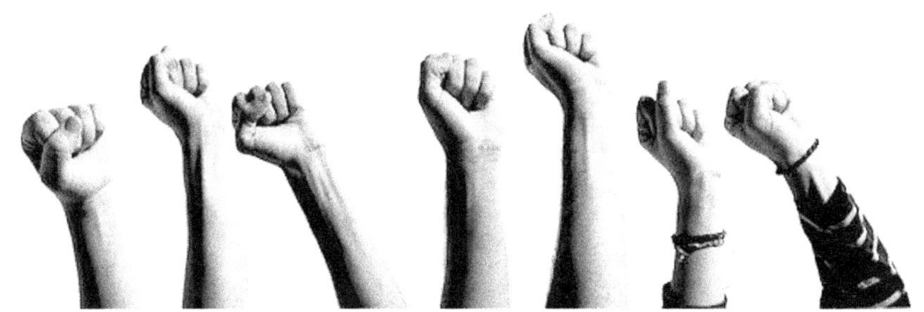

Americans are supposed to be independent, tough, bold, self-reliant, driven by the pioneer spirit and passion for adventure, feisty, sometimes even contrary or rebellious. Nobody pushes us around. We've prided ourselves on our ingenuity and initiative. When the going gets tough, the tough get going. We're the Marlboro Man! We're Wonder Woman!

What the hell happened? When did we lose our confidence?

When did we find it acceptable to cower, surrender, give up hope, give up trying?

I'm not even talking about the average Karen Powderpuff or Joe Sixpack out there. I'm talking about so-called ACTIVISTS!

I see this pathetic negativity, pessimism, insecurity, whiny capitulation, knee-jerk fatalism constantly among the people who are supposed to make reform happen, peace activists dedicated to peace, labor advocates for the working man. Twenty or thirty years ago, I DID NOT SEE THIS COMING. What happened?

To be brutally frank, we don't have time for resignation and surrender. We're just about out of time. The country is a total mess, we're on the verge of financial collapse, the possibility of WWIII and nuclear annihilation are openly and casually bandied about by pundits and politicos, like they're talking about the playoffs for the World Series. It's surreal!

The whole population seems to be slipping into oblivion and paralysis, unable to recognize the decline of the nation or even acknowledge the sinking of their personal fortunes and the diminishing quality of their own lives. Personal credit card debt is now over $1 trillion. Almost 40% of American families can't raise $400 to meet an emergency. People are struggling to pay their student loans and home mortgages. Talk about living on borrowed time!

Of course, you can't put an exact date on a slow, incremental process. The decay and decline are gradual, often imperceptible. But at some point – hopefully before it's too late – people inevitably start to wake up and take stock. The slow boiling frog finally realizes the stew he's in. Folks open their windows and yell: "I'm mad as hell and not going to take it anymore!"

The truth is it's long overdue. To put it bluntly, the complacency of the American public, their willingness to take abuse and be bullied around has gone on way too long. It's appalling. Embarrassing. It's UNAMERICAN!

U.S. history is overflowing with examples of citizens getting fed up, putting their foot down, and demanding an end to abuse of power and exploitation. First and foremost is the rebellion which we celebrate every 4th of July, a courageous, bold act setting the stage for the founding of our nation.

There are many more than most people realize: Shay's Rebellion 1786-87, Whiskey Rebellion 1791-94, Fries's Rebellion 1799-1800, State of Muskogee Tribal Secession 1799-1803, German Coast Uprising 1811, Nat Turner Slave Rebellion 1831, Dorr Rebellion 1841-42, Cherokee Nation Slave Revolt 1842, Anti-Rent War 1839-45, Taos NM Revolt 1847, John Brown Raid on Harpers Ferry 1859, New York City Draft Riots 1863, Battle of Liberty Place 1874, Alabama Election Riot 1874, Greenwood NY Insurrection 1882, Wilmington Insurrection 1898, Green Corn Rebellion 1917, Coal Labor Wars 1890-1930, Battle of Athens TN 1946, San Juan Nationalist Revolt 1950, Black Power Movement 1960s-1980s, Wounded Knee Red Power Movement 1960s-1970s, Attica Prison Riot 1971, Occupy Wall Street 2011, Cliven Bundy Standoff 2014, Occupation of the Malheur National Wildlife Refuge 2016, Seattle Capitol Hill Protest 2020, U.S. Capitol Attack 2021.

Of course, we must include the Civil War (1861-65), which over four years was the bloodiest conflict ever visited on American soil. Additionally, we might throw in several massive "protests", which have made a profound impact on public awareness, and some would argue, still reverberate in our collective consciousness: Vietnam War Protests of 1960s-70s, the Protests Against the War on Iraq 2003, and Black Lives Matter 2013 (ongoing).

The point is that American citizens are hardly strangers to speaking truth to power. Meaning that there's no excuse being squeamish now, especially since we're faced with possibly the worst existential threats to our way of life and the United States of America itself as a nation ever.

Having said that, I recognize that many activists will say: "Speaking truth to power? That's exactly what we're doing!"

I refer them to the riddle: If a tree falls in a forest and no one is around to hear it, did it make a sound?

If we activists are speaking truth to power and no one in power is listening, are we speaking truth to power? Or just talking to ourselves?

I'm not trying to be cute or clever here. I'm drawing much-needed, absolutely essential attention to the central problem with what currently passes for protest and appeals for reform.

NO ONE NOW IN POWER IS LISTENING!

Those now in power are *paid not to listen* to us.

Using logic, facts, moral arguments, appeals to common sense and common decency are a complete waste of time. I repeat …

NO ONE NOW IN POWER IS LISTENING!

So all of the marches, protests, letters to Congress, letters to the editor, petitions, all of it now falls on deaf ears!

Our Congress – even our president – goes to the highest bidder. And against the vast and accelerating fortunes of the tiny class of ultra-wealthy people, not to mention the colossal stockpiles of money accumulated by corporations and their investors, we simply can't compete.

If you stop and think about what I've just said, about how everyone put up by both parties for us to choose from, ultimately end up being slaves to the "donor class", how our system encourages – in fact, incentivizes and richly rewards – our legislators to become pay-for-pay lapdogs to the ruling elite, it explains why, as I pointed out earlier, nothing ever gets done which we the people want done.

It also explains what happened on July 20, 2023 in the congressional hearing which RFK Jr with so much determination and class defended himself. Of course, his fellow Democrats want to destroy him. He wants to level the playing field, have government work to everyone's benefit, he wants to return integrity and fair play to government service, stop the looting of our economy, stop the endless wars and military expansion. He wants an America for all Americans, not just the rich and powerful.

And those sitting up on the dais insulting and interrupting him, making every effort to humiliate and excoriate him, those vile individuals are the foot soldiers for the ruling class, the corporate predators, Wall Street and the big banks, the MIC and warmongers. Their job – and as I said, they are richly rewarded – is to block any real effort on behalf of everyday citizens, to sabotage democracy, to keep the money flowing up up up to the bulging coffers of their donors and paymasters.

Do I have to state again the only conclusion any sane, rational, objective, clear-headed and decent person would come to?

We need to replace those in power – every last one of them – with individuals who will serve and answer directly to us: WE THE PEOPLE!

Yes, we the people have the power.

Yes, it is entirely on our shoulders to make this happen.

Yes, it is our duty and responsibility to put RFK Jr in the White House.

Moreover, and certainly not least …

Yes, it is our duty and responsibility to elect a Kennedy Congress.

It is our duty and responsibility to elect a "people's Congress"!

Nothing else can possibly begin to turn things around.

I hate quoting myself, but it is the core message of this book. This is the only way that Robert F. Kennedy, Jr.'s campaign can make any impact on the future of our country, the only outcome for his and our hard work and noble efforts that will guarantee results:

> "If RFK Jr. is elected in 2024, as a president who reports to the 'people', truly puts the welfare of all of our citizens ahead of Wall Street, the big banks, the military-industrial complex, the ruling elite and other powerful special interests, thus serves the needs of the all citizens, not just the wealthy elite, _HE WILL NEED A CONGRESS THAT SUPPORTS AND PROMOTES HIS GAME-CHANGING AGENDA_."

> "If one of the "bad guys" wins – as has happened for decades, subjecting our nation to economic plunder, endless war, corporate welfare, pay-to-play politics, divide-and-conquer tyranny, thus cheating everyday citizens out of their fair share of our vast national wealth – we will need a Congress that will stop the decline and keep the worst from happening. We'll need a Congress that will end the looting of our economy, the wanton destruction of the environment, the promotion of forever wars and rampant militarization, the marginalization of everyday citizens, the attack on privacy and our human rights, the concentration of wealth in the hands of a tiny elite. _WE WILL NEED A CONGRESS THAT EMBRACES THE VALUES AND GAME-CHANGING AGENDA OF RFK, JR_. We will need a Kennedy Congress!"

Without question, it's a huge challenge. But if people stop arguing over petty differences which in the big picture don't really matter – after all, the survival of America and the greatest experiment in self-government in history are at stake – and unite with a common vision and unyielding determination, we can turn our country around, ushering in a whole new era to bequeath to future generations.

We know what's got to be done.

Let's get to work!

Related Books by John Rachel

If you found this book informative and interesting,
please consider these titles by this same author.

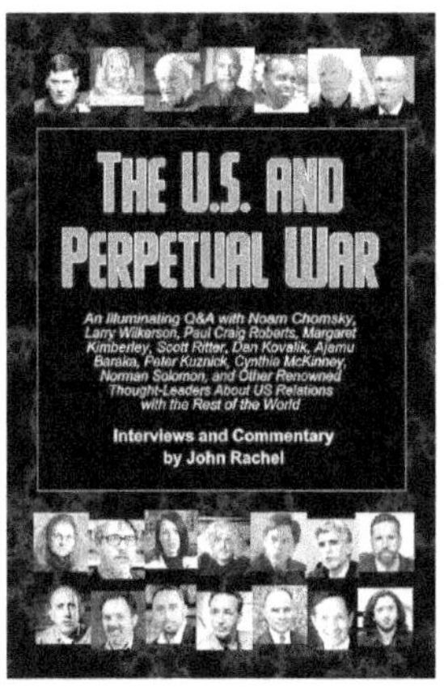

*A powerful and empowering collection of
commentaries and insights by some of today's
most respected political thinkers. Perpetual war
is destroying our nation. To stop the unfolding
disaster, we must honestly look at how our own
leadership and policies have led the country astray.
This book is the perfect place to start.*

Amazon (Kindle): bit.ly/3YSF0OP
Amazon (Print): bit.ly/3qNuqfn
Direct from printer: bit.ly/3PcTJRr
Barnes & Noble: bit.ly/3PcLTXZ
Apple iBook: bit.ly/3QQqC7K
Smashwords: bit.ly/3EePWgk

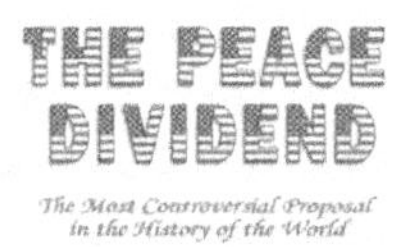

*The Peace Dividend strategy is a direct attack on America's
systemic addiction to war by appealing to the self-interest of
its citizens. The Peace Dividend concept literally
INCENTIVIZES citizens to redirect their thinking and
start WORKING FOR PEACE!
This short book explains how we put America
back on a path of peace and prosperity.*

Amazon (Kindle): amzn.to/2cpIRfQ
Amazon (Print): amzn.to/2cEhnCb
Direct from printer: bit.ly/2c3mJsl
Barnes & Noble: bit.ly/2cWxvzd
Apple iBook: apple.co/2cqw7an
Smashwords: bit.ly/2cb6Cse

In this political drama, a bright, young, idealistic, Green Party candidate in his bid for the congressional seat of a conservative district in Ohio, teams with a beautiful, fiery African-American intern to combat the slick deceptions and ruthless tactics of a sweet-talking right wing incumbent.

Amazon (Kindle): amzn.to/1jetpiY
Amazon (Print): amzn.to/1lddvsp
Barnes & Noble: bit.ly/1l5FmuG
Direct from printer: bit.ly/3Eip4M4
Apple iBook: bit.ly/1gT2O7w
Smashwords: bit.ly/1fIU3Mq

Prepare to see the future of American democracy! This manifesto offers a detailed, step-by-step plan for cleaning up the corruption in Washington DC. This is electoral reform so radical that in one master stroke, it puts America on the path to a healthy economy and directly addresses its #1 and #2 challenges: the suicidal march to war and the destructive impact of a historically high level of wealth inequality.

Amazon (Kindle): amzn.to/1QJRiNZ
Amazon (Print): amzn.to/1Cuq0du
Barnes & Noble: bit.ly/1GpTTLq
Apple iBook: apple.co/1BXnPcy
Smashwords: bit.ly/1B4DQCp
Kobo: bit.ly/1QETE64

This is a manual for constructive voting in the 2016 election. It presents a concrete plan for wresting control of the country and our democracy back from the rich and powerful and restoring the constitutional mandate of government of the people, by the people, and for the people. It's not just more whining. It's a real plan!

Amazon (Kindle): amzn.to/1VMf2Ft
Amazon (Print): amzn.to/1L9SdIC
Direct from printer: bit.ly/1i7ISFM
Amazon CA: amzn.to/1in513n
Amazon GB: amzn.to/1KfjtQO
Amazon JP: amzn.to/1OMslBG

Coming Soon!

[War Is Making Us Poor]

[The Art of War: The Science of Peace]

About the Author

John Rachel has a B.A. in Philosophy, is a novelist and established political blogger. He has written ten novels, four political and two creative non-fiction books. His political articles have appeared at Nation of Change, Counterpunch, Dissident Voice, Popular Resistance, OpEdNews, Greanville Post, and other alternative media outlets.

Since leaving the U.S. in 2006, he has lived in and explored 34 countries. He now permanently resides in a traditional, rural Japanese community about an hour from Osaka, where he lives with his wife of eleven years. Daily he rides his bicycle through the soybean fields and rice paddies of the surrounding landscape and experiences infinite delight in the ringing of temple bells three times a day by monks at a local Shinto shrine. These days he is mostly immersed in good vibrations.

You can follow his writing and evolution of his world view at:

https://jdrachel.com

You can find his novels and creative non-fiction here:

https://johnrachelauthor.com

Acknowledgements

For over eleven years now, peace and electoral reform have been the focus of my political activism and writing. Neither have been satisfying or promising pursuits. Resistance to new ideas, even among those who claim to be devoted to promoting a peaceful world and true representative democracy, is endemic. Rationalizations and twisted logic rule, as with the "leftists" who myopically buy into the neocon fraud that fighting the Russians in Ukraine is supporting the spread of democratic ideals and opposing megalomaniac tyranny. It's difficult, if not entirely impossible, to have a rational discussion with people who have no grasp of history, are completely misinformed — a polite way of saying 'brainwashed' — are too preoccupied with tribal loyalty to look at facts, and are rendered incapable of objective and balanced analysis. This cerebral anechoic chamber is further shackled by stubborn adherence by activists to legacy methods and tactics, and an antiquated view of the mechanisms of political power. Most current activists, especially in the peace movement, tragically are stuck in the early 70s, while the rest of the world has moved on.

Even so, I've refused to give up pushing my outside-the-box ideas to the deaf, dumb and blind. Does that mean I unconditionally fail Albert Einstein's sanity test?

Through the adversity and setbacks that have populated my best attempts at communicating and working with the remnants of a progressive left, my lovely Japanese wife has remained steadfast in her encouragement and support. Her tempered but timely praise for my persistence and determination has helped immeasurably. For this I am infinitely grateful.

I'm also grateful for the advice and constructive comments which I've been given. Among the individuals who have recently nurtured my political savvy are: Paul Craig Roberts, Daniel Kovalik, Andy Caffrey, Matthew Hoh, Coleen Rowley, David William Pear, William Astore, Oliver Lamm, Scott Ritter, and Richard Wolff.

Legal Notices and Disclaimers

Electing A Kennedy Congress (Forming a Government Which Will Support RFK Jr's Efforts to Remake America in Its Own Image) is an original work protected under international copyright law and registered with the U. S. Library of Congress © John D Rachel 2023.

Respecting the rights under copyright reserved above, no part of this publication may be reproduced, stored in or introduced into a retrieval system, archived, or transmitted, in any form, or by any means (electronic, mechanical, photocopying, recording, or otherwise) without the prior written permission of the copyright owner of this book.

John Rachel's Personal Website

Peace Dividend Website

No Contract No Vote Website